The Incredible Pirate Activity Book

Published in Great Britain in MMXVIII by
Book House, an imprint of
The Salariya Book Company Ltd
25 Marlborough Place, Brighton BN1 1UB
www.salariya.com

ISBN: 978-1-912006-49-6

SALARIYA

SCRIBO   BOOK HOUSE   SCRIBBLERS

1 3 5 7 9 8 6 4 2

A CIP catalogue record for this book is available
from the British Library.

Printed and bound in China.

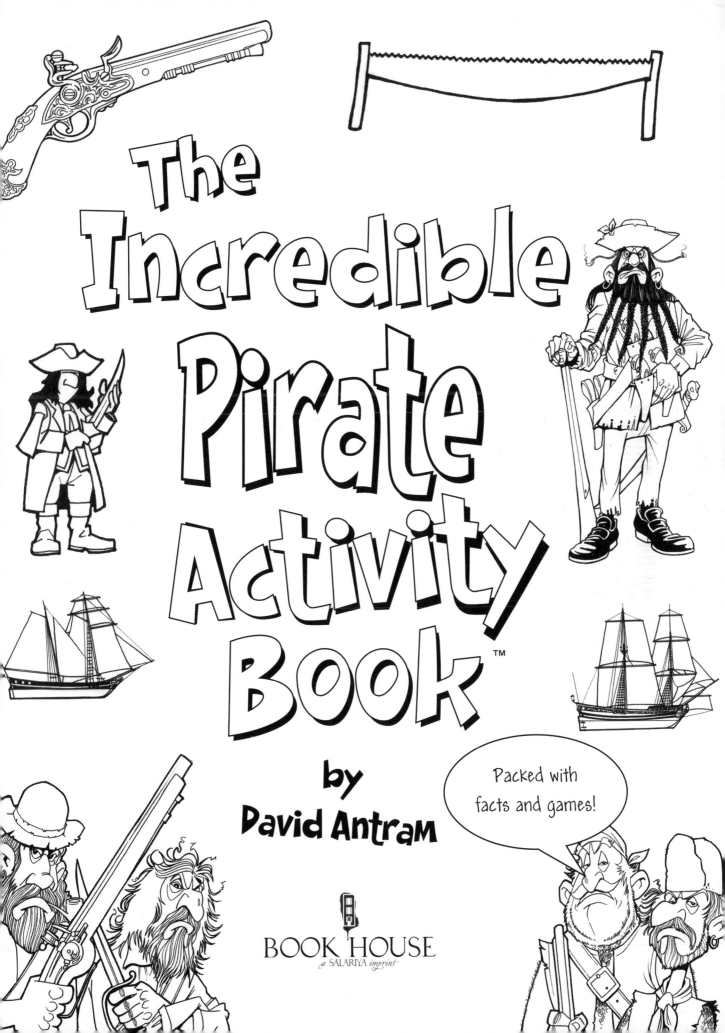

The Incredible Pirate Activity Book™

by
David Antram

Packed with facts and games!

BOOK HOUSE
a SALARIYA imprint

The Jolly Roger

The flag of John Rackham

The Jolly Roger was used as a signal to enemy ships that they were to surrender without a fight. A blood-red flag was more threatening - it signalled that the pirates would show no mercy.

Colour the flags

Colour in these famous pirate flags.

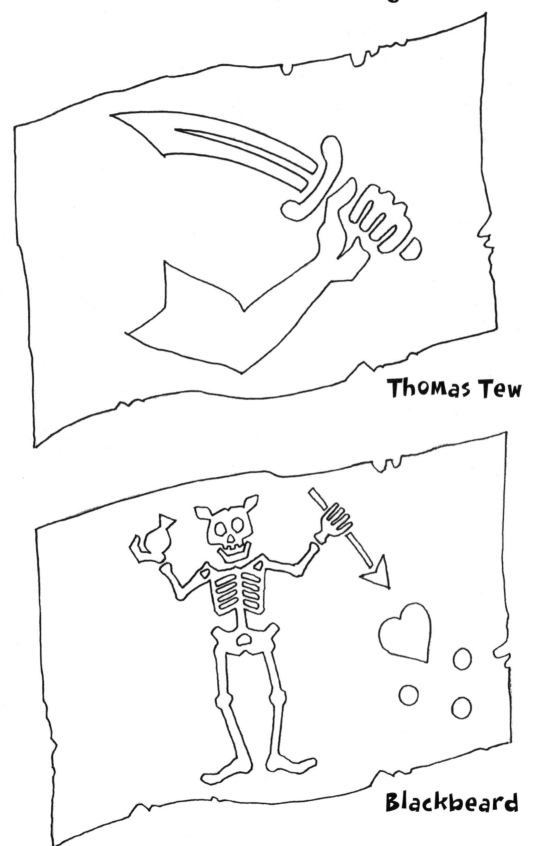

Thomas Tew

Blackbeard

Henry Avery

Bartholomew
Roberts

Design your own flag

Draw your own flag designs in each of these rectangles and then add colour using pencil crayons.

An hourglass was a very popular emblem on pirate flags. Used to symbolise death, the hourglass also had wings to show how quickly time was running out for the pirates' victims.

Blackbeard

Blackbeard was known to fix smoking fuses to his hair and beard before battle. Follow these fuses to see which one is attached to him.

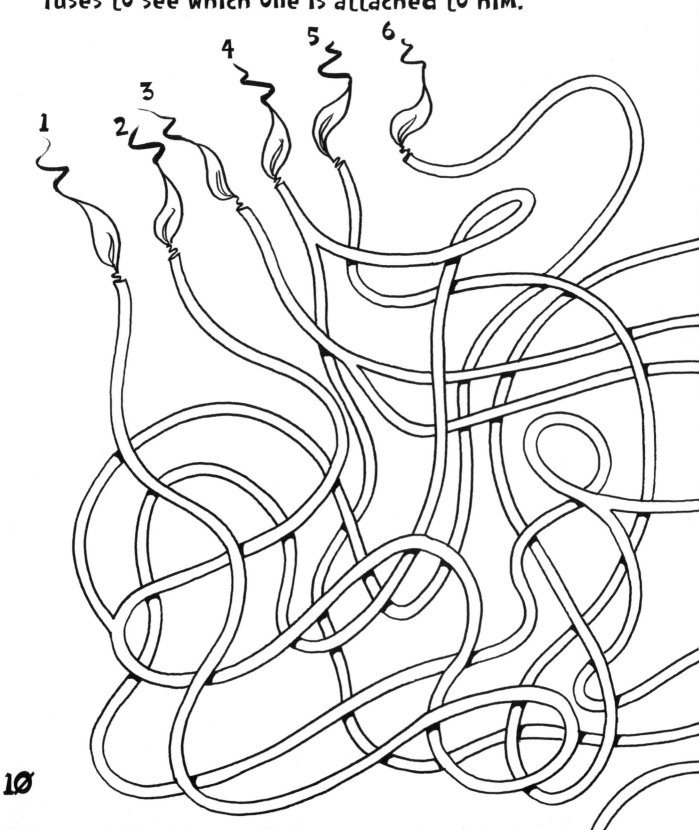

Find the route to Treasure Island

13

Buccaneers

colour in this picture.

14

Buccaneers were runaway slaves,
starving settlers, criminals, pirates and
outlaws. They lived on Hispaniola (now
Haiti) and dressed in homemade, smelly
clothes and blood-stained animal hides.

Black beard

16

Most pirates were murderers but Blackbeard had a different tactic. By making himself look scary enough, he simply terrified his victims into surrendering. Of course, his mighty ship with 40 cannons helped, too!

Build your own pirate

Cut each page (19-26) into three sections along the black lines. Now create some scary pirate faces by mixing and matching them.

Make up your own Pirate faces

Use a black felt-tip pen to draw in noses, eyes, beards, eyepatches etc...

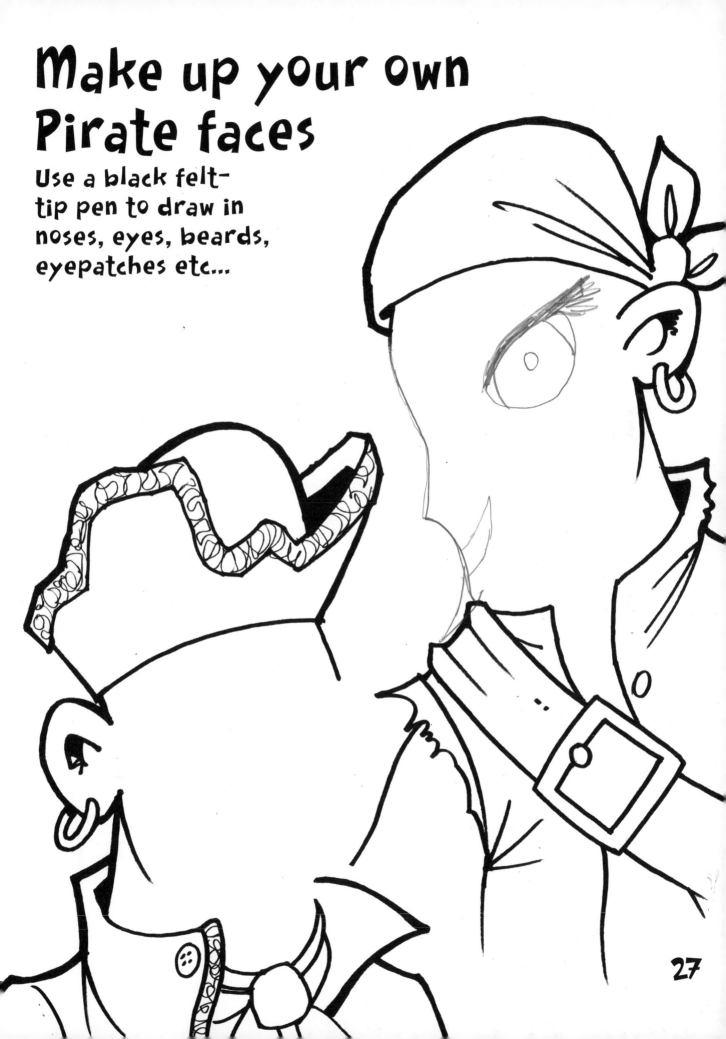

Tattoos

In the early 19th century over 90% of all sailors sported a tattoo. They marked milestones in a sailor's voyage and served as reminders of the places a sailor had been, but mainly they were believed to be talismans to attract good luck.

Spot the only tattoo opposite that matches this one above.

1

2

3

4

5

29

Draw some tattoos on these pirates

Tattoos often had specific meanings: a dragon signified that the bearer had sailed to Asia, a turtle that he had crossed the equator and an anchor that he had crossed the Pacific.

Vikings

colour in this picture.

Design your own Viking shields and colour in the patterns.

33

Sir Francis Drake

Master Mariner, royal favourite and world explorer, Sir Francis Drake rose from humble origins to become England's national hero.
Raised on a houseboat, he learned his seafaring skills from his uncle, a ruthless slave trader. Proud nobles despised Drake, but his courage helped defeat the Spanish Armada in 1588. His privateering exploits won him fabulous riches.

How many words (of three letters or more) can you make from FRANCIS DRAKE?

_____

_____

_____

_____

_____

Privateers

Licensed to raid and kill!
Privateers were raiders
with written permission
from kings, queens or other
powerful people to attack
enemy ships.

Jean Lafitte
(c. 1776-1823)

Caribbean-born Jean
Lafitte raided slave ships,
sold slaves and helped
smugglers.
He also set up a lawless
'pirate kingdom' at
Galveston, Texas.

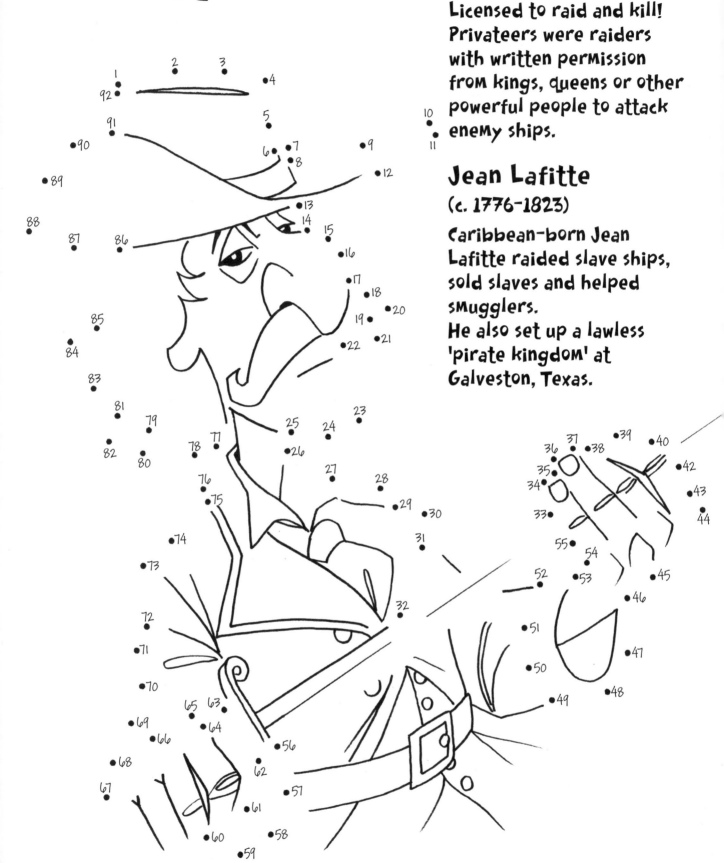

36

William Dampier

Explorer and writer, William Dampier was the first man to circumnavigate the Earth three times.

Pirate attack

38

Join the dots and add colour to the silhouettes.

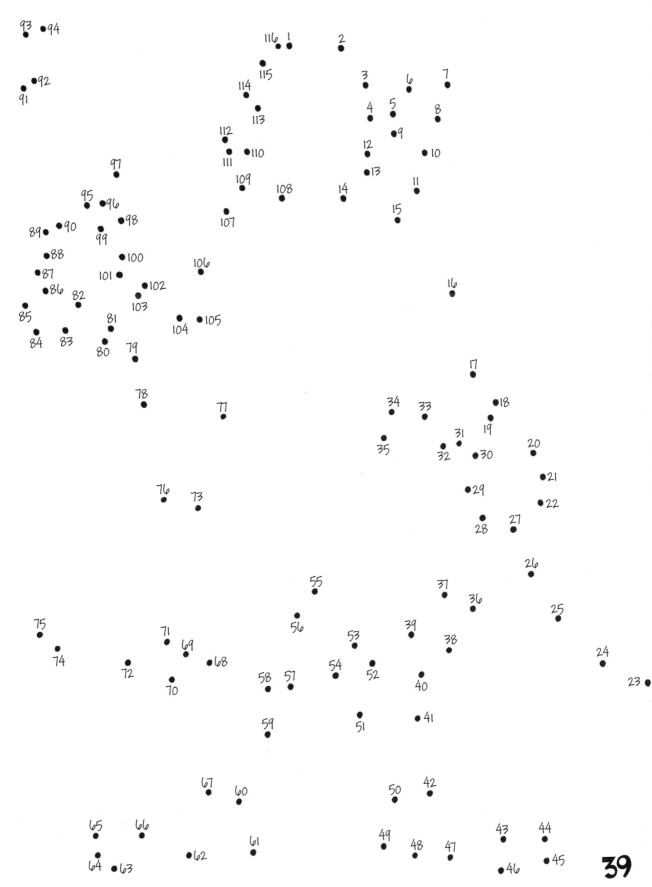

39

Lost Treasure

Burying treasure was uncommon. One of the only pirates known to do so was William Kidd who buried treasure on Long Island before heading to New York City.

Help this pirate find buried treasure...

Henry Avery

A lifelong sailor, Henry Avery first went to sea as a boy with the English navy. Seeking his fortune, he became a slave trader in West Africa, even enslaving the merchants who sold slaves to him. Both a popular and a born leader, Avery became a pirate after leading a mutiny against an English captain.

Colour in all the shapes with dots in them to find how many cutlasses there are on page 43.

43

Land ahoy!

Only two of the islands on the next page match this one. Can you find them?

45

How to draw a pirate captain

Copy this step-by-step pencil drawing

Use simple ovals to draw in the main shapes of Blackbeard's head. Add construction lines for his pirate hat.

Start drawing in his hat and his facial features. Add Blackbeard's eyepatch, beard and moustache.

Draw in more details like the trim on his hat, his eyes, eyebrows, nostrils, ears and earrings. Finally add his teeth and draw in the hairs of his beard.

Use a soft pencil to build up tone by crosshatching.

How to draw a pirate flag

Copy this step-by-step pencil drawing.

Use simple shapes to draw in the basic structure of the skull and crossed swords.

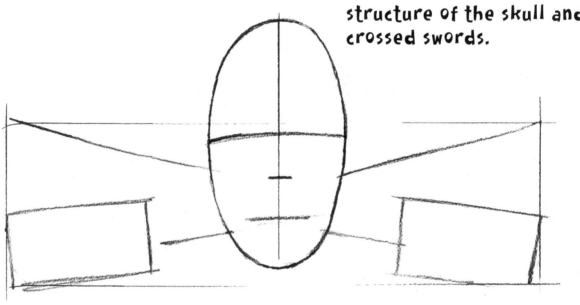

Start drawing in more detail and add facial features to the skull.

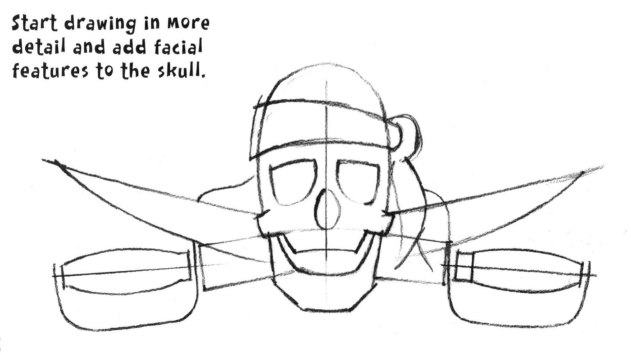

Draw in the teeth, add folds to the bandana and finish off all details. Pencil in some shading.

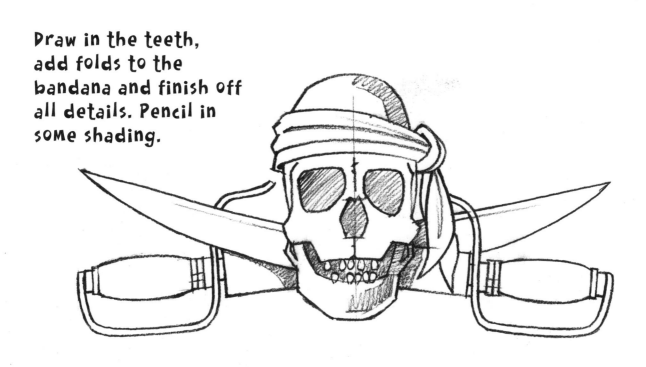

Use a cross-hatching technique to add darker shading - it will create more depth in your drawing.

Anne Bonny and Mary Read

Anne Cormac emigrated to America from Ireland. There, she married James Bonny, a failed pirate and a spy, but she then fell in love with another pirate, 'Calico Jack' Rackham, and ran off with him. Together, they cruised the Caribbean, plundering ships and taking prisoners – including Mary Read – to sell as slaves.

Mary Read dressed as a boy to work as a page and a ship's cabin boy, to earn money for her mother. Still in disguise, she later joined the English army, married a soldier and then helped him run an inn. After his death Mary went back to sea, was captured by 'Calico Jack' and became a pirate.

Add your
own drawings
to finish off
these pictures.

Add your own drawings to finish off these pictures.

Make a treasure Map

Pirates' treasure Maps were More common in fiction than in reality. A 'treasure Map' directs the searcher to the whereabouts of hidden treasure.

YOU WILL NEED:
- 1/2 cup cold tea or coffee
- A sheet of white paper
- Colouring pens or pencils

Draw your own Map by adding...

Skull Mountains
Forest of Doom
Skeleton Beach
etc...

- Tear the edges of your paper to make it look worn (don't use scissors!)

- Crumple it into a ball

- Flatten it out again onto a baking tray

- Pour the tea or coffee over the paper

- Leave it for 5 minutes then drain off (this will make it look 'old')

- Put the paper in the oven for a few minutes until the edges start lifting

- Now start drawing your map!

Mixing lemon juice and water makes invisible ink to mark 'X' for treasure on your map. The 'X' will become visible if you heat it with a hairdrier.

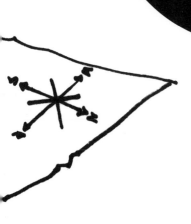

Three easy to Make pirate hats

Cut these hat shapes from thin black card. Cut out a skull and crossbones from white paper and stick on.

Hat One

Cut two identical curved hat shapes out of black card. Glue the corners together as shown. Cut out a skull and crossbones from white paper and stick it on.

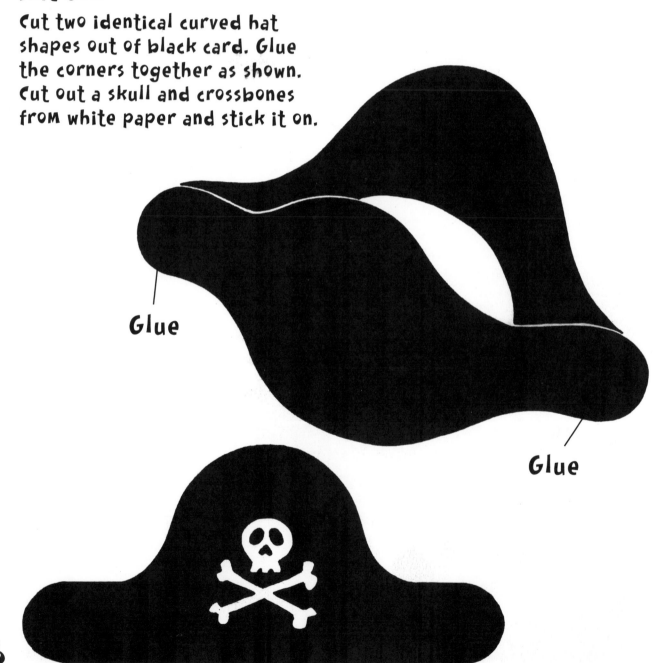

Glue

Glue

Hat Two

Make a paper headband out of thick black card. Cut out a pirate hat shape and glue it to your headband.

Glue

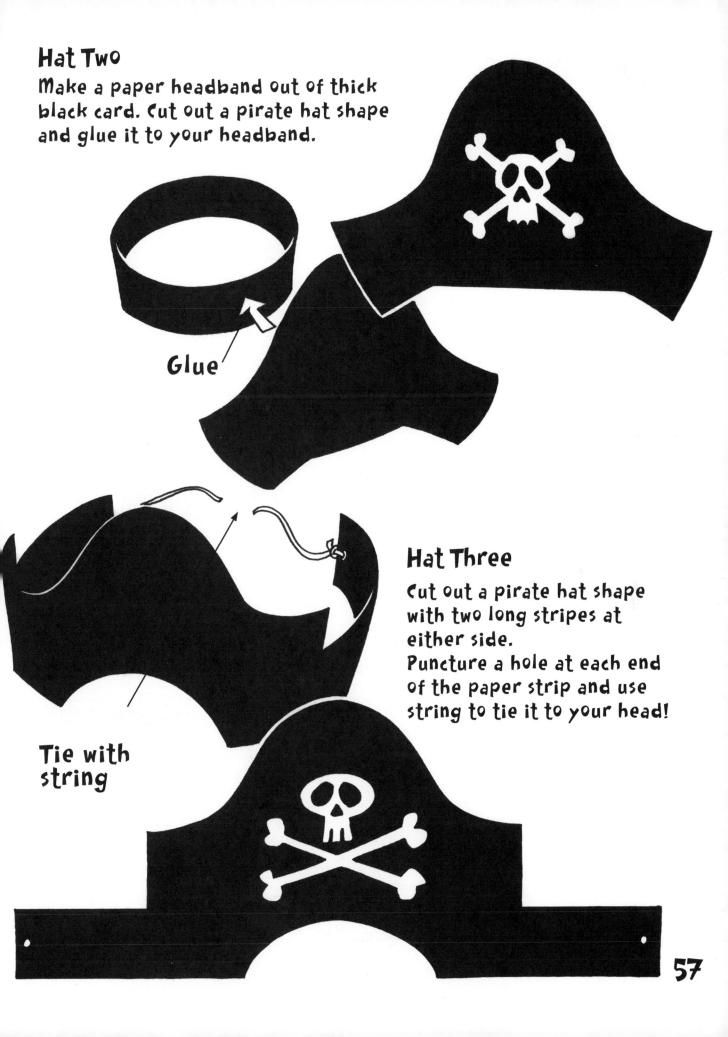

Hat Three

Cut out a pirate hat shape with two long stripes at either side.
Puncture a hole at each end of the paper strip and use string to tie it to your head!

Tie with string

Bartholomew Roberts

Famous for wanting 'a short life and a merry one', Roberts was one of the most successful pirates ever. In just two years, he captured 400 ships, winning 'pleasure, liberty and power' as a result. In spite of his brilliant (and cruel) career, Roberts had not set out to be a pirate. He was originally third mate on a slave trading ship, but was elected captain when its crew mutinied.

Captain Roberts' Rules

1. Fair shares of food and drink for all – and an equal vote on important decisions.

2. Equal shares of plunder for all crew.

3. Cheats to be marooned and onboard robbers to have their noses and ears slit.

4. No gambling, dice or cards.

5. Early to bed – no candles below deck.

Finish off
this picture

59

The Spanish Main

The seas around the Spanish settlements in South America were known as the 'Spanish Main'. Pirates and privateers from many European countries prowled the seas there, eager to attack Spanish treasure ships.

Colour in this Map

A ship's crew

Well-run pirate ships were the most successful ones. Success was achieved by delegating the many different duties required aboard the ship.

Match the job description to the item used:

Quartermaster
As the ship's second-in-command he loves using a cat o' nine tails.

Surgeon
He's quick with a saw, so don't injure a limb or he'll have it off in no time.

Carpenter
He mends the ship's timbers but his skill with a saw means he can do the surgeon's work, too!

Navigator
Using a measuring instrument such as a backstaff, he plots a safe course for the ship to follow.

Cooper
He makes and repairs the ship's wooden barrels, which hold supplies of food and drink.

Ordinary seaman
He keeps the ship in good order: swabbing decks, manning the bilge pumps, working the sails and checking the rigging.

63

Long John Silver

Spot eight differences

'Long John Silver' is the villain in Robert Louis Stevenson's book, 'Treasure Island'.

Weapons

Very few ships put up a fight against pirates! The best way to survive a pirate attack was to avoid a pitched battle. By barricading themselves into the strongest part of the ship, crew members stood the best chance of survival by fighting with homemade bombs!

Fill in the missing letters

B __ m __

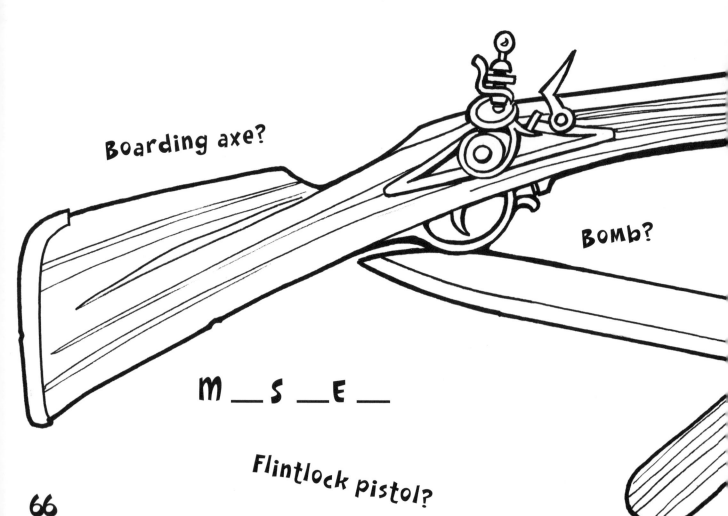

Boarding axe?

Bomb?

m __ s __ E __

Flintlock pistol?

F _ I _ T _ O _ K   _ I _ T _ L

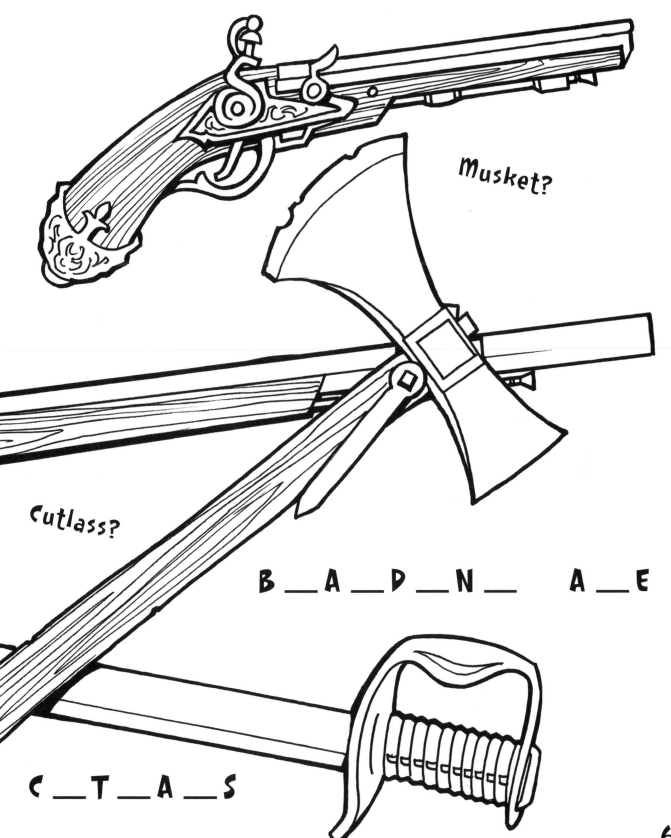

Musket?

Cutlass?

B _ A _ D _ N _   A _ E

C _ T _ A _ S

The Barbarossa brothers

Copy each square of this grid onto the opposite page to recreate the picture below.

68

The Barbary pirates were the most famous and successful of all the pirates who roamed the Barbary Coast of North Africa. They won wars against Christian Spain, conquered kingdoms for Turkey, and helped thousands of refugees escape to safety.

Pirate Ships

Look at these different types of pirate ship

Square Rigger
One of the most aerodynamically-efficient ships.

Schooner
The foremast is much shorter than the mainsail. This ship was popular with pirates for its speed and agility.

Brigantine
A large, two masted ship, that could endure great distances over heavy seas.

Sloop
A small lightweight vessel that cut quickly through the water - perfect for surprise attacks!

Battleships

YOU WILL EACH NEED:
- 2 grids (see page 72)
- A black pen
- A red pen

Battleship Rules (2 players)

1. Both players have two grids. Each player must secretly place (either horizontally or vertically) a Square rigger, a Brigantine, a schooner and two sloops on one grid. Use the key below to see how many squares each type of ship should fill.

2. Players take turns to call out a 'co-ordinate' (a letter and a number) to guess where their opponent's ships are placed. Your opponent checks their grid, and shouts 'hit' if you have guessed correctly and 'miss' if not.

3. Keep a record of all your guessed co-ordinates on your spare grid. Use black for a 'miss' and red for a 'hit'.

4. The first player to sink all his enemy's ships is the winner.

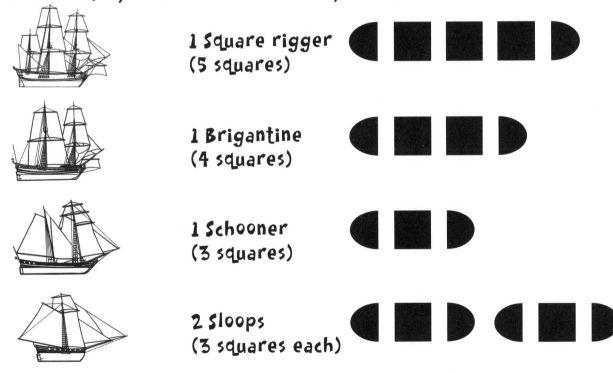

1 Square rigger
(5 squares)

1 Brigantine
(4 squares)

1 Schooner
(3 squares)

2 Sloops
(3 squares each)

Battle Grid

	1	2	3	4	5	6	7	8	9	10	11	12	13	14	15
A															
B															
C															
D															
E															
F															
G															
H															
I															
J															

Spare Grid

	1	2	3	4	5	6	7	8	9	10	11	12	13	14	15
A															
B															
C															
D															
E															
F															
G															
H															
I															
J															

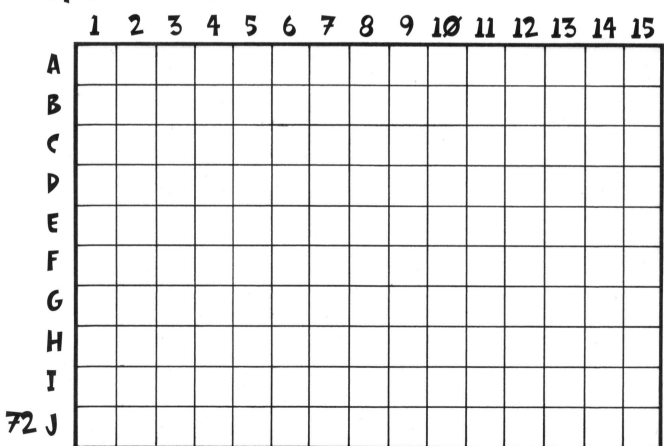

The Dragon Lady

When Shi Xianggu's husband, Zheng Yi, died in a tropical storm, she took over his pirate empire and his name, becoming Zheng Yi Sao. Her fleet of ships terrorised the South China Seas, robbing, destroying and demanding taxes. In 1810, the Chinese government pardoned Zheng Yi Sao for her crimes, and she gave up piracy forever.

Chinese pirates sailed in converted junks (cargo vessels) that were ideal for fighting. They were fast, seaworthy, armed with cannons, and had large holds to store gunpowder.

75

Learning the ropes

Everyone had to know their knots. Pirates had to know how each rope on the mast and sails was tied. A loose knot could end in disaster!

Sheet Bend
to join ropes together

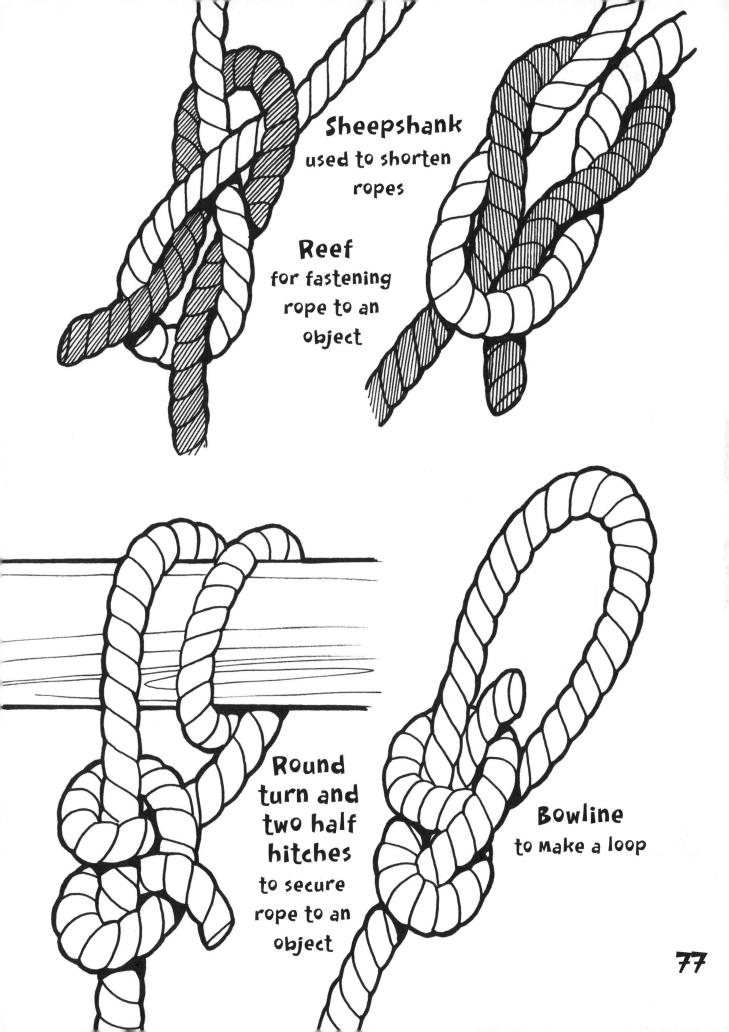

Sheepshank
used to shorten ropes

Reef
for fastening rope to an object

Round turn and two half hitches
to secure rope to an object

Bowline
to make a loop

77

Wordsearch

Find the names of these famous
pirates in the wordsearch

Mary
Read

Anne
Bonny

Blackbeard

Bartholomew
Roberts

Henry Avery

Captain Kidd

Zheng Yi Sao

Henry
Morgan

A	B	V	M	A	U	U	S	Y	R	V	A
U	B	L	A	C	K	B	E	A	R	D	R
D	C	W	R	T	S	A	Q	Q	P	P	T
T	X	H	Y	B	S	R	H	E	O	O	H
D	Y	E	R	A	E	T	E	F	C	N	O
A	N	N	E	B	O	N	N	Y	A	R	L
B	F	R	A	G	Z	U	R	Q	P	N	O
A	B	Y	D	A	H	O	Y	P	T	W	Y
R	L	A	N	N	E	O	M	H	A	L	P
T	A	V	N	B	N	M	O	Z	I	M	K
H	C	E	V	H	G	Z	R	F	N	R	L
O	K	R	C	F	Y	H	G	G	K	O	J
L	W	Y	I	E	I	E	A	M	I	B	O
O	C	D	D	J	S	G	N	H	D	I	L
M	X	K	E	G	A	F	F	L	D	N	X
E	B	Y	I	H	O	I	J	A	G	K	X
W	R	O	B	E	R	T	S	I	J	H	Y

colour this picture

to find out who Long John Silver's companion is...

KEY

1 BLACK
2 RED
3 YELLOW
4 GREEN
5 DARK BLUE
6 GREY
7 ORANGE
8 LIGHT BLUE

80

81

Match the bones

Find two bones that match to complete the pirate flag.

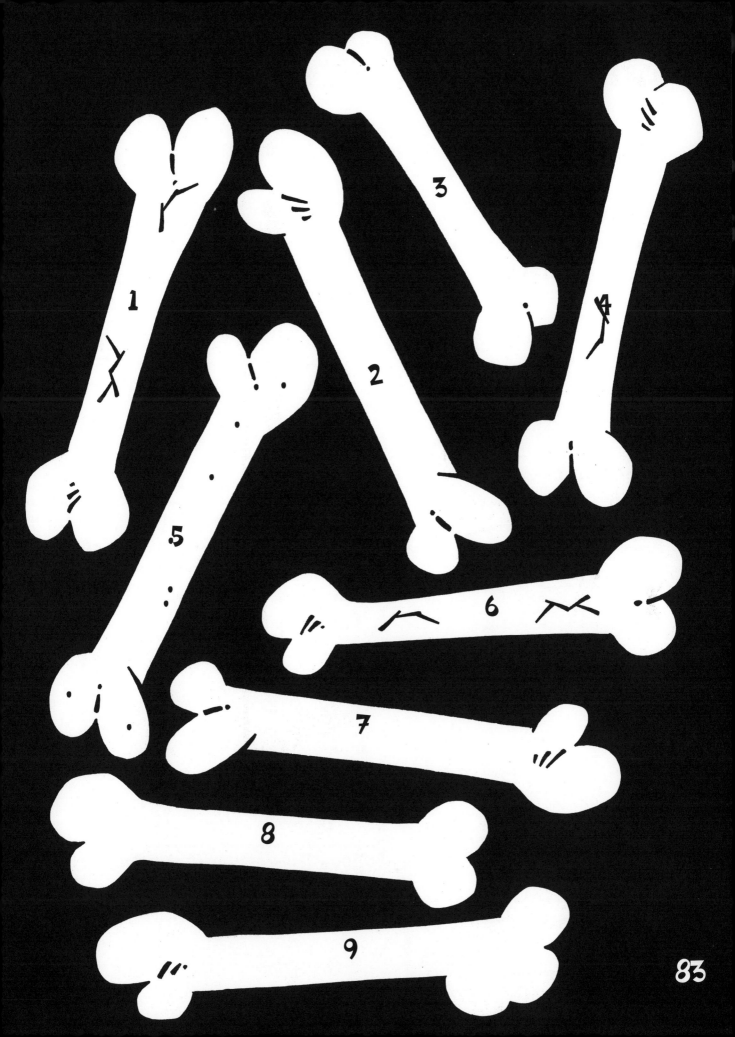

Firing the cannon

Cannons are 3.35 m long and can weigh a deck-smashing 2,040 kg. A 13 cm iron cannonball, weighing 7.7 kg, can be shot about 366 m away.

Colour the pictures

1

Insert charge

Insert a charge of gunpowder packed in a canvas cylinder.

2

Ram it in

Push the charge down to the breech (bottom) of the cannon.

6

Arm the gun
Pour some gunpowder into the touch hole.

7

Take Aim

Move the cannon so it points at the enemy ship.

3 Wad the shot

Pack wadding into the barrel.

4 Load the shot

Roll the cannonball (the shot) down the barrel.

5 Wad the shot

Pack more wadding into the barrel.

8 FIRE

Hold a burning torch at the touch hole and stand back!

BOOM

Sir Henry Morgan

Copy this picture using each square of the grid.

86

Henry Morgan, a privateer, was sent on secret missions by the English to attack and raid Spanish settlements.

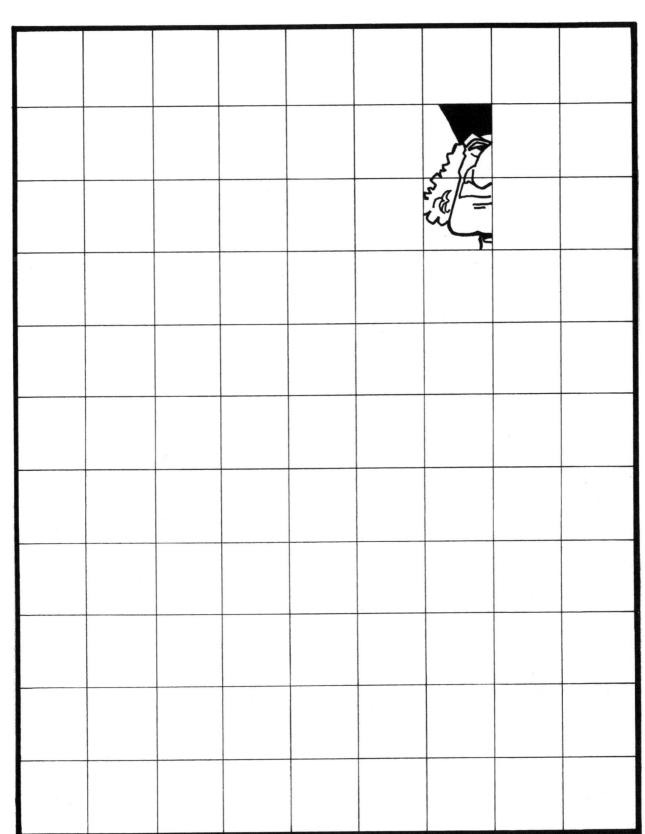

Edward Low

Draw in the missing details on the opposite page.

Edward Low was a notorious English pirate in the 18th century. Born in London, he started thieving at an early age.

Flintlock Pistol

Find the two silhouettes that match the pistol.

3

4

5

6

7

8

Answers

Pages 1Ø-11: Fuse number 4

Pages 12-13:

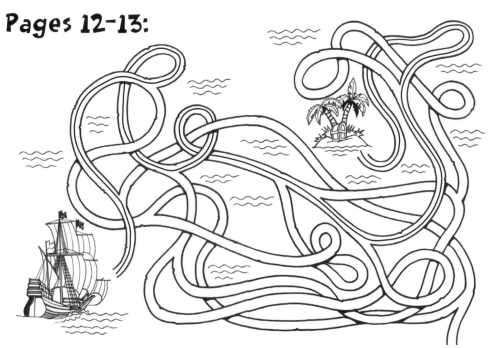

Pages 16-17:

92

Pages 34-35

RANSACKED	SACRED	CARDS	EARN
AIRFARES	FREAKS	FIRED	RISE
RADIANCE	FIENDS	FARES	AREA
REFRAINS	RACERS	FIND	NEAR
CRANKIER	RAINED	FINE	CASE
INFRARED	RADARS	KIND	RICE
SNARKIER	RINSED	CRANE	AID
DRINKERS	RIDERS	DRINK	SIDE
CARRIED	ARCADE	FIRE	END
FRIENDS	CREAKS	FRIED	CARE
RAIDERS	CARIES	EARNS	FIRE
FANCIES	CINDER	NEAR	FAIR
ARSENIC	SAFARI	CAKE	READ
CRANKED	SICKEN	SNACK	SEND
CINDERS	DARKEN	ACID	DISK
SARDINE	DANCER	NAKED	SAFE
SNICKER	DINER	DRIES	RARE
SCARIER	KNEADS	RIDE	RAID
SCARRED	SINCE	ASK	SKIN
SIDECAR	ASKED	CRIED	RACE
DARKENS	RAISE	CREAK	SANK
DANCERS	AREAS	CANE	FAKE
KNIFE	ACRES	SKIED	SAD
DISCERN	FEARS	KNIFE	ACE
ERRANDS	FACES	CASE	
RAISED	RAIN	CARS	
AFRAID	ASIDE	DARE	
RANKED	IDEAS	DICE	
RISKED	DRAIN	SAID	

Pages 40-41:

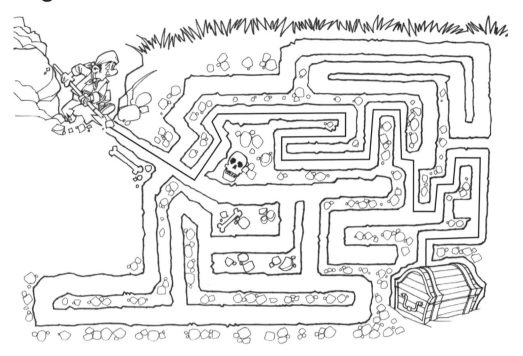

Pages 42-43: Six cutlasses

Pages 44-45: Islands 4 and 5

Pages 62-63:

Carpenter

Navigator

Surgeon

Quartermaster

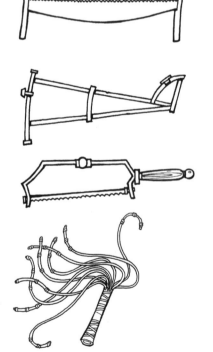

Ordinary seaman

Cooper

Pages 64-65:

Pages 66-67:   BOMB   BOARDING AXE
                    MUSKET   CUTLASS
                    FLINTLOCK PISTOL

Pages 78-79:

A	B	V	M	A	U	U	S	Y	R	V	A
U	B	L	A	C	K	B	E	A	R	D	R
D	C	W	R	T	S	A	Q	Q	P	P	T
T	X	H	Y	B	S	R	H	E	O	O	H
D	Y	E	R	A	E	T	E	F	C	N	O
A	N	N	E	B	O	N	N	Y	A	R	L
B	F	R	E	G	Z	U	R	Q	P	N	O
A	B	Y	D	A	H	O	Y	P	T	W	Y
R	L	A	N	N	E	O	M	H	A	L	P
T	A	V	N	B	N	M	O	Z	I	M	K
H	C	E	V	H	G	Z	R	F	N	R	L
O	K	R	C	F	Y	H	G	G	K	O	J
L	W	Y	I	E	I	E	A	M	I	B	O
O	C	P	D	J	S	G	N	H	D	I	L
M	X	K	E	G	A	F	F	L	D	N	X
E	B	Y	I	H	O	I	J	A	G	K	X
W	R	O	B	E	R	T	S	I	J	H	Y

95